IN  JIS

CARS AND VEHICLES

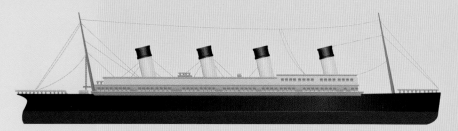

First published in paperback in Great Britain
in 2021 by Wayland
Copyright © Hodder and Stoughton, 2018
All rights reserved

Executive editor: Adrian Cole
Produced by Tall Tree Ltd
Editor: Jon Richards
Designer: Ed Simkins

ISBN: 978 1 5263 0696 8

Wayland
An imprint of Hachette Children's Group
Part of Hodder and Stoughton
Carmelite House
50 Victoria Embankment
London EC4Y 0DZ

An Hachette UK Company
www.hachette.co.uk
www.hachettechildrens.co.uk

Printed and bound in China

FSC
www.fsc.org

MIX
Paper from
responsible sources
FSC® C104740

GETTING ABOUT 4

THE WHEEL 6

ON YOUR BIKE! 8

CARS AND TRUCKS 10

TRAINS 12

BOATS AND SHIPS 14

PADDLES AND SAILS 16

SUBMARINES AND SUBMERSIBLES 18

INTO THE AIR 20

LIGHTER THAN AIR.....................................22

PLANES.. 24

HELICOPTERS 26

THE FUTURE...28

GLOSSARY 30

INDEX..32

GETTING ABOUT

If you want to get from one place to another then you need the right vehicle. You can't fly in a boat and you can't travel underwater in a plane, so you've got to make sure that what you're travelling in is up to the job.

Q: What's your vehicle like?

A: A car is designed to travel over land. It has a number of wheels (round ones, of course!) and a body, called a chassis. This has to hold the engine, driver, passengers and load – it can be a tight squeeze!

A: A plane has wings to lift it off the ground (without flapping) and a body to carry the pilots, passengers and cargo.

A: A boat is designed to float (not sink!) and travel through the water. It has a pointed shape so that it can move as easily as possible.

Aerodynamics

So you've chosen what vehicle you want – but is it really the right shape? An object that does not have an aerodynamic shape will create tiny currents of air behind it. These create a force called drag, making the object harder to move. An aerodynamic object reduces the amount of disturbance in the air, reducing drag.

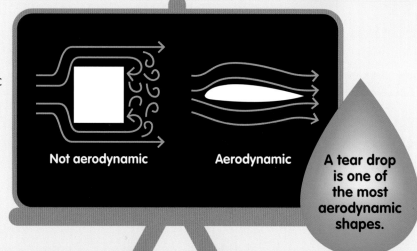

Not aerodynamic

Aerodynamic

A tear drop is one of the most aerodynamic shapes.

Power source

Different vehicles use different power sources to push them along.

Some cars use electric motors to push them along.

Many cars use internal combustion engines to power them.

If you need to get into space, then a rocket engine is the power source for you!

It's getting a bit crowded up here!

Planes and superfast cars use jet engines and even rockets to blast them along.

One more puff and we're home.

Or you could just rely on the wind to blow you across the blue ocean ...

In January 2017, the yacht *IDEC3* captained by Francis Joyon set a world record for sailing around the whole planet in just **40 days, 23 hours, 30 minutes and 30 seconds.**

5

THE WHEEL

Wheels help to make the world go around! They are found on most land vehicles and make it easier for them to roll from one place to another. Without them life, travel and motion would be a lot harder.

Big wheels, small wheels
Wheels can be found on the smallest vehicles, such as prams and scooters, right up to the biggest, such as trucks and diggers.

Q: What is a wheel?

Wheel

Wheel

Axle

A: That's easy! A wheel is made up of a round disc that rotates around or with an axle.

The **Bagger 293** is one whopper of a vehicle. It is **225 metres long** and **weighs 14,200 tonnes**. At its front is a **huge cutting wheel** which is **21.3 metres across** – taller than 12 adults.

Cutting wheel

How wheels work

A wheel rotates around an axle. Because the wheel is rolling over the ground and not dragging along it, the friction between the wheel and the ground is much lower. The only significant amounts of friction are between the wheel and the axle.

What a drag!

Simply dragging an object along the ground requires a lot of effort, because friction between the two surfaces is very high. Wheels work by reducing this friction.

Why do they make these things so hard to move?!

High friction

Low friction

Changing wheels

The earliest wheels were made from solid, heavy pieces of wood.

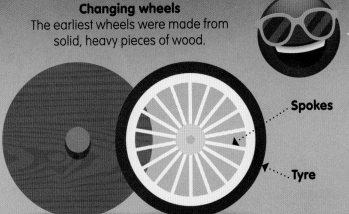

Modern wheels are made from lighter materials, such as metal alloys, and have spokes to make them even lighter. They also have tyres to improve grip and make the ride smoother, so you can roll over the road nice and easy.

Spokes

Tyre

ON YOUR BIKE!

When you push on a bike's pedals, the force is transmitted through the chain and to the back wheel. Turning the pedals moves the chain, which turns the bike's wheel.

Handlebars
– used to steer the bike

Changing gear affects how easy it is to move the bike and how fast you can go.

Front wheel

High gear
What happens – higher ratio between pedal gear and wheel gear means the back wheel moves more for each turn of the pedal.
What it's used for – moving quickly.

Low gear
What happens – smaller ratio between pedal gear and wheel gear means the back wheel turns less for each turn of the pedal wheel. **What it's used for** – moving away from a standing start, climbing steep hills.

The longest bike in the world measures 35.79 metres – as long as three buses.

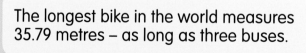

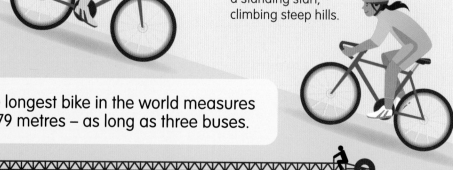

Frame – keeps the bike together and usually made from metal tubes

Saddle – where you sit!

Brakes – to slow you down or stop

Back wheel

Chain – transmits force to back wheel

Pedals – Where the real work happens

Q: When was the bicycle invented?

A: The earliest pedalled, two-wheeled cycles appeared in the 1860s. They were so uncomfortable to ride that they were nicknamed 'bone shakers'.

In May 2017, American cyclist Amanda Cocker set a new record for the distance cycled in one year, covering 139,269 km **– equivalent to three-and-a-half times around the world.**

x3½

To slow down, you squeeze the brake levers which pull on cables that are linked to callipers on the front and back wheels.

The callipers squeeze rubber brake pads into the rims of the wheels or onto discs attached to the wheels. This increases the friction, slowing the wheels down and making the brakes hot.

CARS AND TRUCKS

Today, our roads are teeming with millions of cars and trucks. But these vehicles are only a little more than 100 years old, and they have changed greatly since they first appeared.

Q: Who invented the car?

A: That was me, Karl Benz, and I invented the modern car or automobile. I patented my three-wheeled 'Motorwagen' in 1886.

KARL BENZ

But hang on, Mr Benz! Cars were around long before you appeared on the scene.

In the early 1500s, Leonardo da Vinci sketched an idea for a horseless, powered cart – it was never built.

Frenchman Nicholas-Joseph Cugnot built an artillery wagon in 1769 that was powered by steam.

In the 1830s, two inventors, Scotsman Robert Anderson, and American Thomas Davenport, both developed the first electric cars.

In 1899, Camille Jénatzy zoomed to one of the earliest land speed records in **an electric car** called *La Jamais Contente*, reaching **100 kph**.

Thrust SSC

La Jamais Contente

Today's **land speed record** stands at **1,227.985 kph** and was set in 1997 by British pilot Andy Green in **Thrust SSC**.

Hydrogen fuel cells may be the future of powering cars and trucks, but they were invented by British scientist William Grove way back in 1839 …

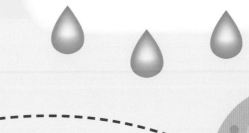

… the only exhaust they produce is water vapour.

On 18 October 1984, Emil and Liliana Schmid from Switzerland set out in their car on a journey. By April 2017, they had covered **741,065 km** – that's **almost the distance to the Moon and back!** All in the same car! And they're still going!

But there aren't any roads up here!!

One of the world's biggest dump trucks is the **BelAZ 75710**. It is 20.6 m long and 8.165 m tall. It can carry a load of **450 tonnes** …

… that's the weight of four blue whales!

TRAINS

Whether it's steam, diesel, electric or even magnetic, trains have been carrying people and cargo from one place to another along tracks and rails for hundreds of years.

Parts of a train

Some electric trains collect the current from overhead wires using a pantograph.

Pantograph

Overhead wires

Driver's cabin

The tracks are supported by large concrete bars called sleepers.

The wheels are arranged in groups of four or six, known as bogies.

Trains usually run along two parallel tracks.

The USA has about 240,000 km of train track linking the 48 mainland states – **that's enough to go around the world almost six times.**

One rail
A train that runs along one rail is called a monorail.

These train facts will keep you on track!

Mallard holds the record for the fastest steam locomotive in the world. It set the record speed of **203 kph in 1938.**

In **2007**, a French TGV set a record speed of **574.8 kph.**

The record for a manned train was set by a Japanese **LO Series maglev** train. It reached **603 kph in 2015.**

Hold onto your hats! In April 2003, a rocket sled blasted along a set of rails at Holloman Air Force base, USA, to a speed of 10,325 kph, or 8.5 times the speed of sound, setting the record for the fastest speed by a land vehicle.

My name's Richard Trevithick and I invented the first steam-powered locomotive railway. It was set up in 1804 to carry iron ore between the Welsh towns of Merthyr Tydfil and Abercynon.

Q: How can magnets power a train?

A: It's all down to attraction! The like poles of magnets repel, or push each other away. Magnets on the train and the track repel each other, causing the train to float above the track. Other magnets then push and pull the train along the track. With no friction between the train and the track, maglev trains can zoom along at incredible speeds.

RICHARD TREVITHICK

13

BOATS AND SHIPS

Boats come in all shapes and sizes depending on what they have to carry and how far they travel. While early boats and ships were made from wood, today's vessels are made from metals and ultra-light composite materials.

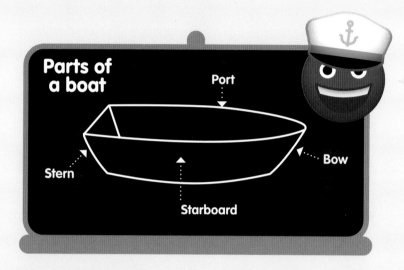

Parts of a boat

Port

Stern

Bow

Starboard

Ship shape
Ahoy there! Boats usually have a pointed front, called the bow so they can move easily through the water.

Many hulls make light work
The body of a boat is called the hull. But some boat designers aren't happy with just one hull, oh no! Some boats have two or even three hulls. These reduce the contact area with the water so the boats can move more easily.

Q: Who is the speed king on the water?

A boat with one hull is called a **monohull**.

A boat with two hulls is called a **catamaran**.

A boat with three hulls is called a **trimaran**.

A: In 1978, Australian Ken Warby blasted his jet-powered speed boat *Spirit of Australia* to **511 kph** to set the world water speed record.

Giant ships over the years

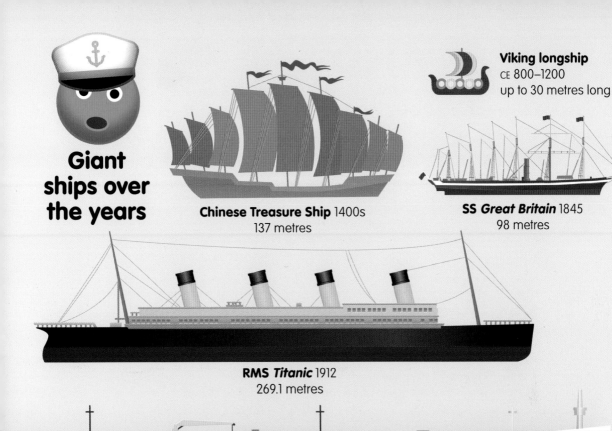

Chinese Treasure Ship 1400s
137 metres

Viking longship
CE 800–1200
up to 30 metres long

SS *Great Britain* 1845
98 metres

RMS *Titanic* 1912
269.1 metres

Seawise Giant (supertanker) 1979
458.45 metres

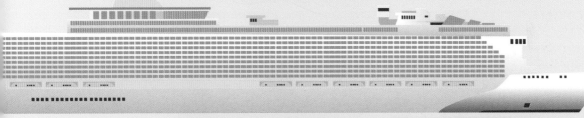

MS *Harmony of the Seas* (biggest cruise liner) 2016
362.12 metres

Set on its end, the *Seawise Giant* would be taller than the Empire State Building (381.01 metres).

Super-strong ships
Heavy-lift ships are special ships designed to carry rigs and other ships if they are damaged.

Early ships were made from wood. HMS *Victory*, launched in 1765, used 6,000 mature trees.

HMS *Warrior* became the world's first iron-hulled warship when it was launched in 1860.

PADDLES AND SAILS

So you've launched your boat and ship and it floats (which is good!). But how do you get it to move about? Do you choose wind, engines or just paddle it yourself?

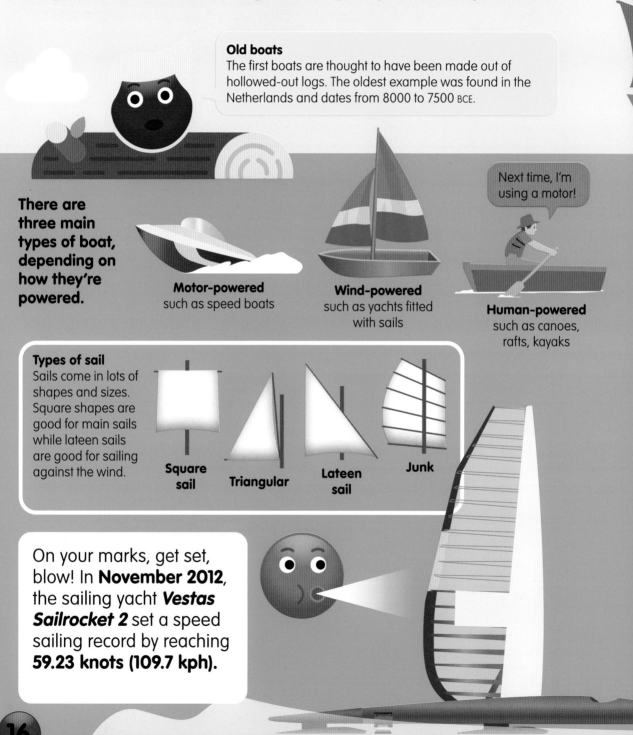

Old boats
The first boats are thought to have been made out of hollowed-out logs. The oldest example was found in the Netherlands and dates from 8000 to 7500 BCE.

There are three main types of boat, depending on how they're powered.

Motor-powered
such as speed boats

Wind-powered
such as yachts fitted with sails

Next time, I'm using a motor!

Human-powered
such as canoes, rafts, kayaks

Types of sail
Sails come in lots of shapes and sizes. Square shapes are good for main sails while lateen sails are good for sailing against the wind.

Square sail

Triangular

Lateen sail

Junk

On your marks, get set, blow! In **November 2012**, the sailing yacht **Vestas Sailrocket 2** set a speed sailing record by reaching **59.23 knots (109.7 kph)**.

Enormous sailing ships

Built for the naval expeditions of the Chinese admiral Zheng He in the 1400s, Chinese treasure ships were huge vessels measuring 137 m long, more then twice the size of the largest European ships from the period.

Giant propeller

When it comes to shifting cargo, bigger is better! The *Emma Maersk* is a container ship that is fitted with some of the largest propellers ever made. Each bladed wheel measures 9.6 metres across – that's nearly the height of 6 adults.

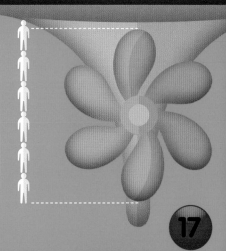

HMS *Rattler*

HMS *Alecto*

Tug of war

In March 1845, HMS *Rattler* took part in a tug-of-war contest with HMS *Alecto* to see which was better – paddle wheels or propellers. The propeller-powered *Rattler* won the day, pulling the paddle-powered *Alecto* back at 2 knots (3.7 kph).

SUBMARINES AND SUBMERSIBLES

Take a deep breath and join us on a journey beneath the waves. Today's submarines can sail around the world without coming to the surface, while submersibles can withstand the crushing pressures of the deep.

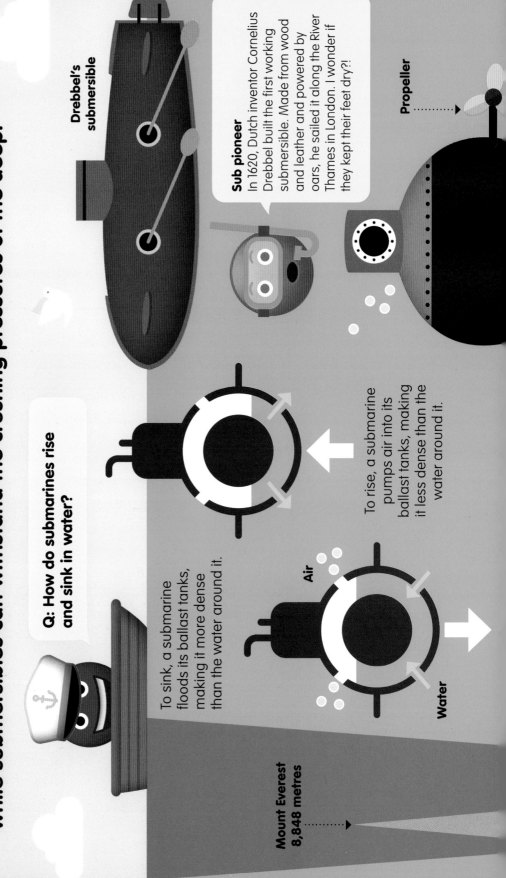

Drebbel's submersible

Sub pioneer
In 1620, Dutch inventor Cornelius Drebbel built the first working submersible. Made from wood and leather and powered by oars, he sailed it along the River Thames in London. I wonder if they kept their feet dry?!

Propeller

Q: How do submarines rise and sink in water?

To rise, a submarine pumps air into its ballast tanks, making it less dense than the water around it.

Air

Water

To sink, a submarine floods its ballast tanks, making it more dense than the water around it.

Mount Everest 8,848 metres

Turtle

Attack sub

In 1775, American engineer David Bushnell built the world's first military submersible. *Turtle* was powered by a hand-cranked propeller and designed to sail under enemy ships and attach explosives.

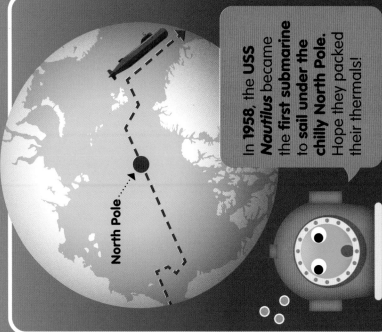

In **1958**, the **USS *Nautilus*** became the **first submarine** to **sail under the chilly North Pole.** Hope they packed their thermals!

North Pole

A world-record dive needs a very special submersible. And that's exactly what *Deepsea Challenger* is. I usually direct blockbuster movies, but on 26 March 2012, I piloted this submersible to the bottom of Challenger Deep in the Pacific Ocean, reaching a depth of 10,908 metres.

JAMES CAMERON

Deepsea Challenger

Come and look at my pretty light!

Challenger Deep 10,916 metres

INTO THE AIR

While humans have always dreamed of flying like birds, it's only been in the last 250 years that we've really been able to get our feet off the ground.

Don't get too close
Greek legend tells the story of Icarus and his father Daedulus, who built wings made from feathers and wax to escape from the island of Crete, where they were being held prisoner. However, Icarus flew too close to the Sun, which melted the wax in his wings and he fell to his death.

Should have packed my parachute!

Early balloons
The first living creatures to fly in a hot-air balloon were a duck and a chicken in September 1783.

I thought you could fly, anyway!

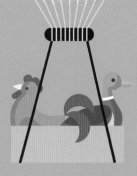

The Montgolfier brothers built the first balloon to carry people. This historic flight took place on **21 November 1783** with Jean-François Pilâtre de Rozier and the Marquis d'Arlandes on board.

On **17 December 1903, Orville Wright** made the **first powered flight** in a heavier-than-air plane. The flight lasted for **12 seconds** and covered just **37 metres** – about half the wingspan of a **Boeing 747 Jumbo Jet.**

Call that a flight!

FLIGHT PIONEERS

On 25 July 1909, I became the first person to fly across the English Channel.

In May 1932, I became the first woman to fly solo non-stop across the Atlantic. Five years later, though, I disappeared while trying to fly around the world.

It took us 14.5 hours to make the first flight across the Atlantic Ocean on 14 June 1919.

LOUIS BLÉRIOT

CAPTAIN JOHN ALCOCK
and
LIEUTENANT ARTHUR BROWN

AMELIA EARHART

LIGHTER THAN AIR

Up, up and away! Hot-air balloons and airships use a large bag, called the envelope, which holds the gases that lift them into the air.

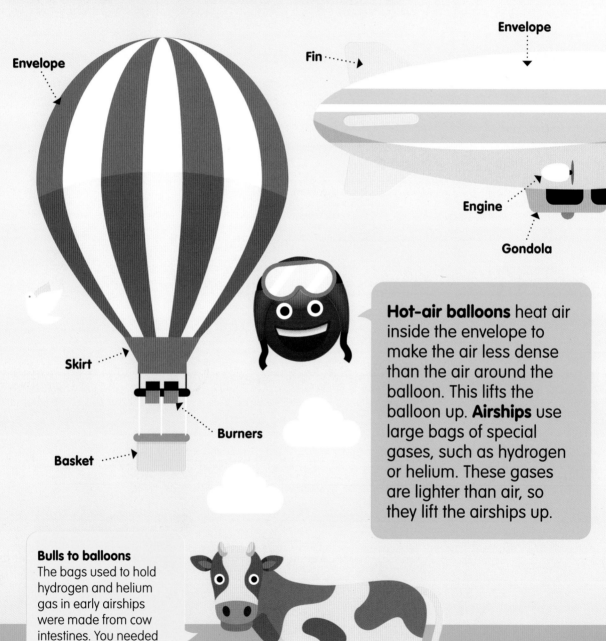

Envelope

Fin

Envelope

Engine

Gondola

Skirt

Burners

Basket

Hot-air balloons heat air inside the envelope to make the air less dense than the air around the balloon. This lifts the balloon up. **Airships** use large bags of special gases, such as hydrogen or helium. These gases are lighter than air, so they lift the airships up.

Bulls to balloons
The bags used to hold hydrogen and helium gas in early airships were made from cow intestines. You needed the intestines from 250,000 cows to make a single Zeppelin airship.

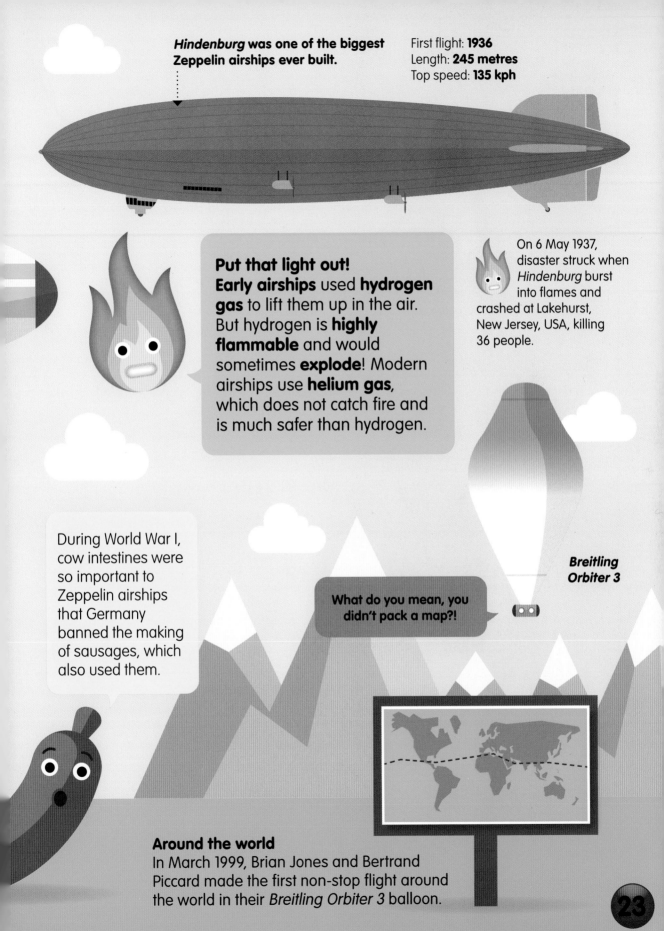

Hindenburg was one of the biggest Zeppelin airships ever built.

First flight: **1936**
Length: **245 metres**
Top speed: **135 kph**

Put that light out!
Early airships used **hydrogen gas** to lift them up in the air. But hydrogen is **highly flammable** and would sometimes **explode**! Modern airships use **helium gas**, which does not catch fire and is much safer than hydrogen.

On 6 May 1937, disaster struck when *Hindenburg* burst into flames and crashed at Lakehurst, New Jersey, USA, killing 36 people.

During World War I, cow intestines were so important to Zeppelin airships that Germany banned the making of sausages, which also used them.

What do you mean, you didn't pack a map?!

Breitling Orbiter 3

Around the world
In March 1999, Brian Jones and Bertrand Piccard made the first non-stop flight around the world in their *Breitling Orbiter 3* balloon.

PLANES

All a plane needs to get in the air is an engine and a couple of wings. Sounds simple? But things are a little more complicated than that!

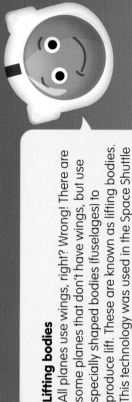

Lifting bodies

All planes use wings, right? Wrong! There are some planes that don't have wings, but use specially shaped bodies (fuselages) to produce lift. These are known as lifting bodies. This technology was used in the Space Shuttle and in designs for future spaceplanes, such as Dream Chaser.

Dream Chaser

Getting in the air

Air moving over a wing has lower pressure than air moving below the wing.

The wing is angled upwards, which deflects air down, pushing the wing up.

The angle of the wing is known as the angle of attack.

Lower pressure

Higher pressure

Wing

Higher pressure below the wing pushes the wing up.

Straight wings create a lot of lift and are used on high-flying or slow-moving planes, such as gliders and spy planes.

Swept back or delta wings are used on very fast aircraft, such as fighter planes.

Q: What shape is a wing?

A: The shape of a wing depends on how the aircraft is to be flown.

The **Antonov An-225** has six engines and is one of the heaviest and longest aircraft ever built. Designed as a cargo plane, it can carry up to **250 tonnes of cargo** – more than the weight of **two blue whales or 30 elephants!**

Keep flapping! They'll think we're birds!

Antonov An-225

The Boeing 787-9 Dreamliner has a range of 14,140 km and sips fuel, using just **3.08 litres per 100 km per seat.**

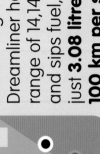

787-9 Dreamliner

Concorde

Atlantic Ocean

Faster than sound

Concorde was a supersonic jet airliner that could fly at more than twice the speed of sound and cross the Atlantic in a little more than 3 hours.

Dreamliners and fuel efficiency

The future is light and efficient! The latest jet airliners are built from composite, super-lightweight materials and can cover huge distances without having to refuel.

HELICOPTERS

Helicopters are incredibly useful aircraft. They can fly backwards and forwards, hover in mid-air and land and take off vertically. This means they are able to fly to and land at places that planes can't reach.

Parts of a helicopter

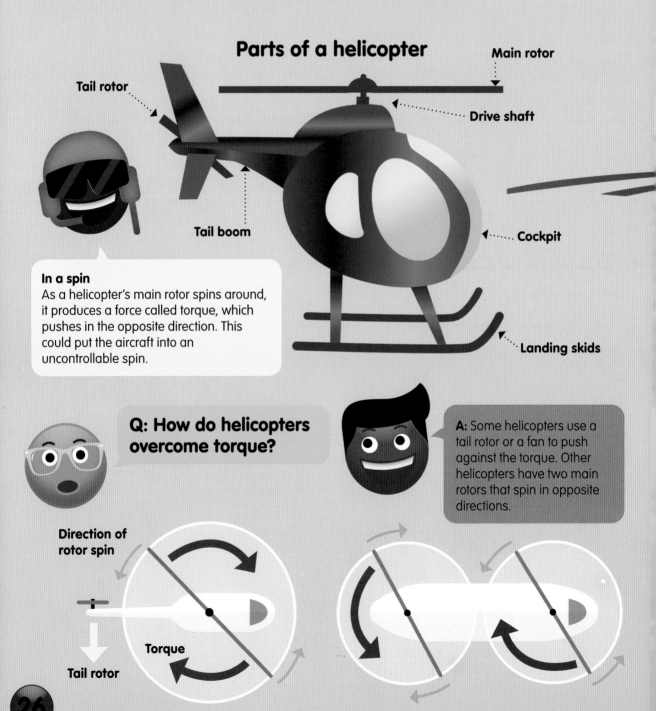

Main rotor

Tail rotor

Drive shaft

Tail boom

Cockpit

In a spin
As a helicopter's main rotor spins around, it produces a force called torque, which pushes in the opposite direction. This could put the aircraft into an uncontrollable spin.

Landing skids

Q: How do helicopters overcome torque?

A: Some helicopters use a tail rotor or a fan to push against the torque. Other helicopters have two main rotors that spin in opposite directions.

Direction of rotor spin

Torque

Tail rotor

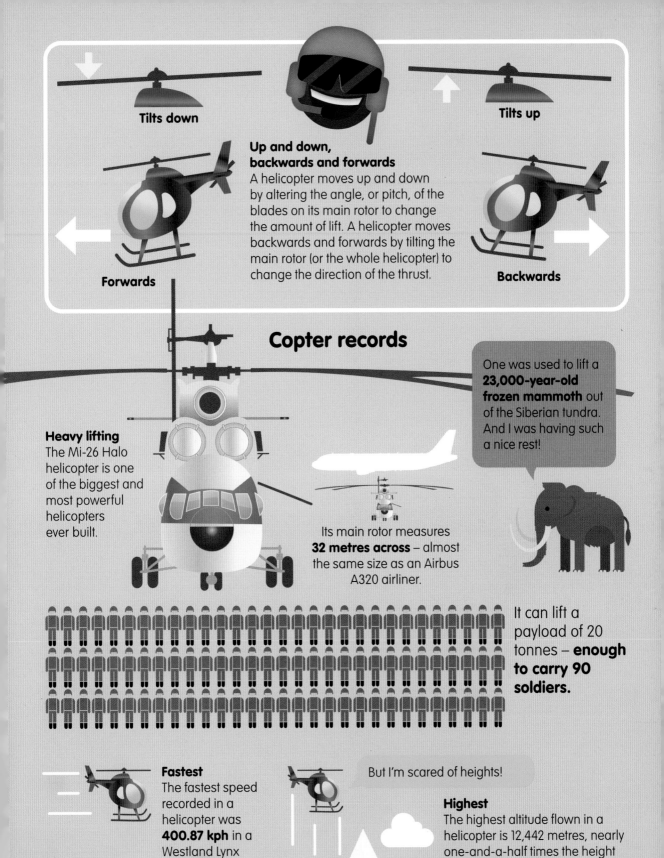

Tilts down

Tilts up

Forwards

Backwards

Up and down, backwards and forwards

A helicopter moves up and down by altering the angle, or pitch, of the blades on its main rotor to change the amount of lift. A helicopter moves backwards and forwards by tilting the main rotor (or the whole helicopter) to change the direction of the thrust.

Copter records

One was used to lift a **23,000-year-old frozen mammoth** out of the Siberian tundra. And I was having such a nice rest!

Heavy lifting
The Mi-26 Halo helicopter is one of the biggest and most powerful helicopters ever built.

Its main rotor measures **32 metres across** – almost the same size as an Airbus A320 airliner.

It can lift a payload of 20 tonnes – **enough to carry 90 soldiers.**

Fastest
The fastest speed recorded in a helicopter was **400.87 kph** in a Westland Lynx achieved in August 1986.

But I'm scared of heights!

Highest
The highest altitude flown in a helicopter is 12,442 metres, nearly one-and-a-half times the height of Everest, in an Aérospatiale SA 315B Lama in June 1972.

27

THE FUTURE

Whether it's super-speedy trains, space-cargo launchers, or the reappearance of an early form of transport, scientists and inventors are always looking to see how they can make travel faster and more efficient for all of us.

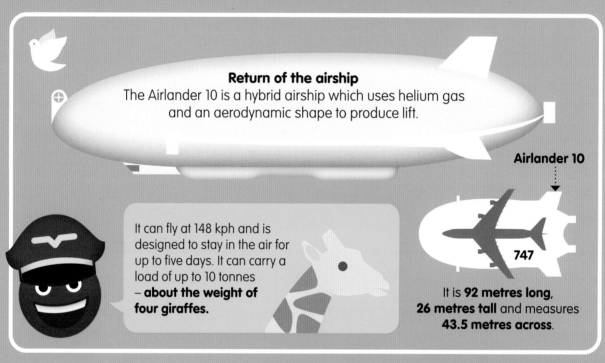

Return of the airship
The Airlander 10 is a hybrid airship which uses helium gas and an aerodynamic shape to produce lift.

Airlander 10

It can fly at 148 kph and is designed to stay in the air for up to five days. It can carry a load of up to 10 tonnes – **about the weight of four giraffes.**

747

It is **92 metres long, 26 metres tall** and measures **43.5 metres across**.

The Hyperloop

Self-driving cars

Information is analysed by a computer to adjust steering, acceleration and braking.

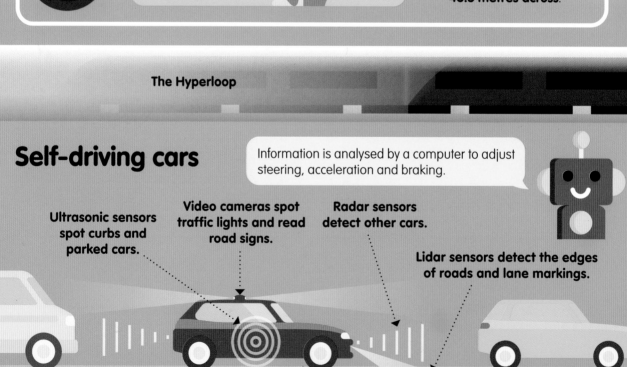

Ultrasonic sensors spot curbs and parked cars.

Video cameras spot traffic lights and read road signs.

Radar sensors detect other cars.

Lidar sensors detect the edges of roads and lane markings.

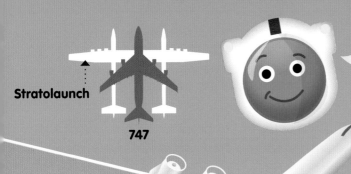

Stratolaunch

747

Spaceplane
The six-engined 'Stratolaunch' is designed to carry satellites high into the atmosphere from where they can blast into orbit. This huge plane has a wingspan of 117 metres – longer than a football pitch.

Are you sure this thing has got enough engines?!

Q: What do you get if you cross a vacuum cleaner with a high-speed train?

A: The Hyperloop.

The Hyperloop will feature long, low-pressure tubes along which passenger carriages will zoom. With reduced air pressure, carriages can zip along easily and quickly and are designed to reach speeds of **up to 1,200 kph.**

A trip from Los Angeles to San Francisco (560 km) would take just 35 minutes!

This is one way to get above it all!

Straddle buses
This idea saw large passenger buses driving 4–5 metres above normal traffic using rails on either side of the road. A prototype was designed and tested in China, but later scrapped after the government withdrew its support.

GLOSSARY

AERODYNAMIC
A vehicle that is aerodynamic can move through the air or water quickly and easily.

AXLE
A rod running through the centre of a wheel and around or with which the wheel rotates.

BOW
The front of a boat or ship.

CALLIPERS
Two arms that are hinged together so that they can open and close. Some brake mechanisms use callipers to squeeze brake pads against a wheel or a brake disc.

CATAMARAN
A boat with two hulls.

COMPOSITE
A material that is made up of two different substances.

DELTA WINGS
A wing that is shaped like a triangle and is usually fitted to fast aircraft. Its name comes from the Greek letter 'delta', which is shaped like a triangle.

DIESEL
A heavy oil that is used as the fuel in a diesel engine.

DRAG
A force that acts against the direction of movement as an object moves through air or water.

FRICTION
A force created when two objects rub against each other, making things difficult to move.

GEARS
Toothed wheels that are used to transmit a force, increasing or decreasing the amount of energy needed to produce motion.

HULL
The body of a boat or ship.

INTERNAL COMBUSTION
Used to describe a type of engine that produces energy by burning a fuel, such as petrol, inside itself.

JET
A type of engine that mixes fuel and air and ignites the mixture to produce a blast of hot gases that roar out of the back of the engine and push a vehicle forwards.

LATEEN SAIL
A triangular-shaped sail.

LIDAR
A device that detects the position or movement of objects using laser radiation.

LIFT
A force produced when air or water passes over a specially shaped object. The force acts at right angles to the direction the air or water is flowing in.

MAGLEV
Short for 'magnetic levitation' this uses a system of magnets to raise a vehicle off the ground or rails, reducing friction and allowing it to move quickly and easily.

PANTOGRAPH
A sliding, diamond-shaped device that is fitted to the tops of trains and trams and is used to collect electricity from overhead cables.

PORT
The name given to the left side of a boat or ship.

ROCKET
A type of engine that mixes a fuel with oxygen in either solid or liquid form and sets light to the mixture to produce a blast of hot gases. These gases roar out of a nozzle at the back of the vehicle, pushing the vehicle forwards.

SPOKES
Bars that connect the outer rim of a wheel to its centre.

STARBOARD
The right side of a ship.

STERN
The rear of a boat or ship.

SUBMERSIBLE
A small vehicle that can go underwater.

TORQUE
A force that causes something to turn around a central point, such as an axle.

TRIMARAN
A boat or ship with three hulls.

TYRES
A piece of rubber that is fitted to the outside of wheels.

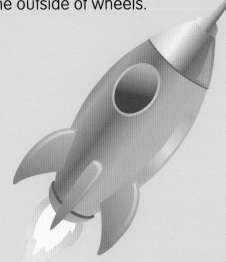

INDEX

aerodynamics 4
airships 22, 23, 28
Alcock, Captain James 21
alloys 7
axles 6, 7

Benz, Karl 10
bikes 8–9
Blériot, Louis 21
boats and ships 4, 5,
    14–15, 16–17
bow 14
brakes 9
Brown, Lieutenant Arthur
    21

callipers 9
Cameron, James 19
cars 4, 5, 10–11, 28
catamaran 14
chains 8, 9
chassis 4
composite materials 14,
    25

drag 4

Earhart, Amelia 21
electric cars 10
electric motors 5

frame 9
friction 7, 9

gears 8, 9

handlebars 8
heavy-lift ships 15
helicopters 26–27
hot-air balloons 20, 22, 23
hulls 14
hydrogen fuel cells 11

internal combustion
    engines 5

jet engines 5

land speed record 10
lifting bodies 24

maglev trains 13
monohull 14
monorails 12

North Pole 19

paddle wheels 17
pantographs 12
pedals 8, 9
planes 4, 5, 21, 24–25
propellers 17

rockets 5, 13
rotors 26, 27

saddles 9
sails 16
speed sailing record 16
spokes 7
steam trains 13
submarines and
    submersibles 18–19

torque 26
tracks 12
trains 12–13, 28
Trevithick, Richard 13
trimaran 14
trucks 10, 11
tyres 7

water speed record 14
wheels 4, 6–7, 8, 9
wings 4, 24